A Vision of Pastoral Ministry

✠ ✠ ✠

Richard R. Gaillardetz, Ph.D.

Liguori
ONE LIGUORI DRIVE
LIGUORI MO 63057-9999

Imprimi Potest:
Richard Thibodeau, C.Ss.R.
Provincial, Denver Province
The Redemptorists

ISBN 0-7648-0771-4
Library of Congress Catalog Card Number: 2001098538
© 2002, Liguori Publications
Printed in the United States of America
02 03 04 05 06 5 4 3 2 1

Scripture quotations are from the *New Revised Standard Version of the Bible,* © 1989 by the Division of Christian Education of the National Council of Churches of Christ in the USA. Used with permission. All rights reserved.

Portions of the following text have been previously published as (*Worship*, September 1993), "In Service of Communion: A Trinitarian Foundation for Christian Ministry," and as the keynote address, entitled "To Teach of the Trinity," to the 2000 convention of the National Conference of Catechetical Leadership.

To order, call 1-800-325-9521
www.liguori.org
www.catholicbooksonline.com

Contents

✠ ✠ ✠

Introduction / 5

Imagining God / 7

God as a Remote Superbeing / 10
God as the Superabundance of Love / 17
Imago Dei: We Are Made
   for Communion / 23

**Pastoral Ministry: Serving the
Life of Communion / 29**

The Minister as Mystagogue / 29
The Minister as Contemplative Witness
   to Life / 39
The Minister as Prophet / 44
The Minister as a Compassionate and
   Healing Presence / 52
The Minister as a Person of Hope / 58

Conclusion / 62

About the Author

Dr. Richard R. Gaillardetz holds the Margaret and Thomas Murray and James J. Bacik Endowed Chair in Catholic Studies at the University of Toledo in Toledo, Ohio. He has published numerous articles and authored or edited five books, including *A Daring Promise: A Spirituality of Christian Marriage* (Crossroad, 2002). He is currently a Catholic delegate on the U.S. Catholic-Methodist Dialogue and past (2000) recipient of the Washington Theological Union's Sophia Award, offered in recognition of "theological excellence in service to ministry." Dr. Gaillardetz is a popular speaker at theological and pastoral conferences and is married and the father of four young boys.

Introduction

✠ ✠ ✠

In the four decades since the opening of Vatican II, the Church has experienced a great flowering of ministries. Here in the United States, the Church has largely embraced Vatican II's reaffirmation of the dignity of all the baptized and their right and responsibility to participate in the life of the Church. Many parishes have witnessed a marvelous flourishing of ministries, some undertaken by paid professionals but many others performed by those who simply responded to their baptismal call without any financial remuneration. The development of these ministries has been a great blessing for our Church. However, in our national tradition for pragmatic action, our practice has tended to run ahead of our reflection. Because it can be dangerous to act without grasping the deep significance of our actions, it may be helpful to explore the theological and spiritual foundations for what we do as pastoral ministers.

I would like to begin with an exploration of two great themes that run throughout our Christian tradition. The first is that our God is encountered, in Jesus and by the power of the Spirit, as the Superabundance of Love. The second is that we humans are created in the image and likeness of God and therefore discover ourselves when we are able to participate in the Superabundance of Love, which is the very life of God. In the second part of this booklet, I will explore how these themes can help us better understand the work we do as pastoral ministers.

Imagining God

✠ ✠ ✠

Almost all Christians would profess belief in the doctrine of the Trinity. However, not only do few understand the doctrine, but few even *expect* to understand it. As many a perplexed priest, parent, and catechist has solemnly intoned, "After all, it is a *mystery*!" But you know, it really isn't a mystery. God is the one, truly incomprehensible Mystery. Church doctrine is supposed to help illuminate, in an imperfect way, something vital, something fundamentally true about that God who is Mystery. So when we dismiss as mystery any doctrine, but particularly one as central as the Trinity, we are robbing ourselves of an opportunity to deepen our understanding of who this God is who comes to us as Word and Spirit. As the *General Directory for Catechesis* notes:

> *The presentation of the innermost being of God, revealed by Jesus, the mystery of being one in essence and three in Person, has vital implications for the lives of human beings....The human and social implications of the Christian concept of God are immense.[1]*

For so many, the "human and social implications" of this doctrine are lost behind a haze of lofty speculation that seems remote from the daily lives of believers. Yet, if we cut away all of the technical theological language, the doctrine of the Trinity is fundamentally about the way we imagine God in relation to our own lives.

Our Catholic tradition has a wonderful intellectual heritage in which some of the most brilliant minds humankind has ever known have employed their gifts to offer some real and meaningful insight into the nature and being of God. A broad list of technical jargon has emerged to bring out these insights. Unfortunately, this highly cognitive approach generally finds expression in the formulation of clear and precise truth statements about God. This has created two difficulties. First, the development of the technical jargon has had the effect of limiting God-talk to the professionals—the theologians and clerics. Ordinary believers have often been scared away by their sense of inadequacy in the face of this highly developed intellectual discourse. Second, the emphasis on precise truth statements has led to the neglect of the role of the imagination, the way in which our belief in God is shaped by stories and images as much as by technical, propositional statements.

Think about religious disagreements that you may have had with friends, family, or even members of your faith community. Have you ever found yourself in that odd situation in which you share a common belief system (for example, you both believe in Jesus or in the importance of the sacraments) but yet seem still to be talking past one another? I am convinced that many of our most significant religious disagreements are not about doctrine but about something more basic—different ways of imagining God. Put simply, many Christians who would profess the same faith and the same religious doctrines use their imaginations to bring that faith to life in fundamentally different ways. They operate out of different models, different imaginative constructs of how God is related to the world. Let me propose two such models.

God As a Remote Superbeing

The more common view of God and God's relationship to us starts from the assumption that God is another individual being within the great cosmos. In this model, the distinction and the distance between God and the world is stressed. This model draws on a wide range of metaphors. God is King and Ruler, Lord, Master of the Universe, Father-Patriarch. This set of metaphors illuminates God's power and sovereignty but can also encourage the view of God as an individual superbeing residing in heaven.

These images of God can still be very helpful to our spiritual life, but they were originally used within the framework of a biblical faith that gave them a distinct meaning. In ancient Judaism, God's people were convinced that God was irrevocably bound to them in covenant, and they experienced God continually pouring forth mercy and blessings from the depths of divine love. The people of Israel knew their God to be God-for-us. Early Christians moved easily within this biblical faith but professed that this God of the covenant was encountered in a unique and unsurpassable way in Jesus of Nazareth by the power of God's Spirit. The doctrine of the Trinity emerged over several centuries in the early Church, not as a set of abstract postulates but as a formal expression of their experience of the encounter with Jesus of Nazareth, God's Word definitively spoken into human history and received in the Spirit.

In later centuries, this understanding of the Trinity as an expression of the Christian experience of the God of salvation would be eclipsed. It was gradually replaced by abstract speculation about the inner life of God that made the doctrine of the Trinity seem irrelevant to Christian living. God was worshiped as a distant being residing in heaven, not as the God encountered in daily life as Love Unbounded. Things became worse when in the seventeenth and eighteenth centuries the Enlightenment gave rise to the philosophical conviction that all God-talk must submit to the canons of reason and logic. The unintended consequence was the reduction of the biblical God of Jesus Christ to an abstract Supreme Being and First Cause. God would be more and more frequently imagined as an individual being, a divine causal principle radically distinct from the world. Christians would continue to employ traditional terms and images to name their God, but they were not immune to the influence of the Enlightenment and its impact on images of God.

Ironically, Christian fundamentalists, who in the early twentieth century both rejected the central thrust of the Enlightenment and resolutely turned to traditional biblical imagery, nevertheless ended up adopting the basic imaginative framework of the Enlightenment. Though still prayed to as Father, Son, and Spirit, in the imaginations of many Christians God had become a kind of divine

"Santa Claus" who stands outside of our world but is ready to answer our prayers at a moment's notice and step in to make everything better. This view of God as an individual Supreme Being is reflected in the following diagram.

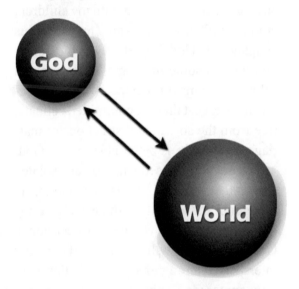

This way of imagining God has come to dominate popular Christian piety with serious consequences for Christian living.

First, if God is an individual being among other individual beings, another individual

in the larger household of all reality, then
God will inevitably have to compete for my
love and attention. My whole life will then
be an endless tug-of-war between the mat-
ters that demand my attention in the daily
course of human affairs—preparing classes,
buying groceries, playing with my children,
talking with my wife—and my religious
obligations to God. Regrettably, in the Catholic tradition some theologies of committed
celibacy assume this perspective and consequently suggest that the committed celibate,
free from the so-called distractions of marriage and family, is better able to love God.

The second consequence of an isolated
God is that, because in this view God is an
individual outside my ordinary world, my
encounter with God will be only occasional.
God-experiences will only be brief episodes
interspersed throughout my life. In this view,
I encounter God only in response to prayer
or through the reception of the sacraments
or some such thing. I understand my life as
essentially profane and godless, punctuated
by brief encounters with the sacred. My spiritual life will be a mad attempt to insert as

many sacred moments as possible into the profane structure of daily life with the hope of thereby sanctifying my life. This episodic spirituality is supported by the "thing-ification" of grace, that is, the tendency to imagine divine grace as a kind of spiritual fuel and the Church and its ministers as sacramental grace dispensers. Decades ago, the late Teilhard de Chardin acknowledged the dominance of this viewpoint. He wrote:

I do not think I am exaggerating when I say that nine out of ten practising Christians feel that [human] work is always at the level of a "spiritual encumbrance." In spite of the practice of right intentions, and the day offered every morning to God, the general run of the faithful dimly feel that time spent at the office or the studio, in the fields or in the factory, is time taken away from prayer and adoration. It is impossible not to work—that is taken for granted. Then it is impossible, too, to aim at the deep religious life reserved for those who have the leisure to pray or preach all day long. A few moments of the day can be salvaged for God, yes, but the best hours are absorbed, or at any rate, cheapened, by material cares. Under the sway of this feeling, large numbers of Catholics lead a double or crippled life in practice: they have to step out of their human dress so as to have faith in themselves as Christians— and inferior Christians at that.[2]

To counter this all-too-common imaginative framework we must recover the deeper insights from our Christian tradition embedded in the doctrine of the Trinity.

QUESTIONS FOR REFLECTION

To what extent has your own spirituality been influenced by this view of God as remote super being?

How does this view of God affect the way we think of the spiritual dimensions of family life and career?

God As the
Superabundance of Love

In the fourth century, the Council of Nicaea taught that the Word incarnate in Jesus was "one in being" (*homoousios*) with the Father. This assertion, fundamental to Christian understandings of the Trinity, did not compromise the belief in God's oneness but rather suggested that as Christians we vision God's unity not as a self-contained individual superbeing but as a God whose very essence is loving relationship. God's unity or oneness is a relational and expansive oneness. The Council recognized that fundamental to the faith of early Christians was their experience of God revealing the depths of covenantal love in the person of Jesus of Nazareth. They experienced Jesus as the concrete expression of God's love for them. They knew the Holy Spirit as both the divine atmosphere in which they encountered Christ and the divine power by which they were brought into communion with God in union with Christ. Emerging Trinitarian doctrine named the *shape* of the Christian encounter with God. God was not a distant entity sending divine intermediaries. Rather, Christians experienced God as the Divine Source and Superabundance of Love being poured forth in Jesus of Nazareth, made effective by the Holy Spirit, and at every moment inviting the believer into trans-formative relationship. The following dia-gram suggests something of this movement.

Father ⟶ Word ⟶ Spirit

Outpouring of Love

Conceiving the triune life of God as a divine movement toward us in love points to the essential insight of Trinitarian doctrine, namely that God's very being, what it is for God to be, is loving, life-giving relationship. God does not just *have* a love relationship with us, God *is* loving relationship. This means that an imaginative view of God's relationship to us must resist thinking of God as an individual being whose grace must be imported into our world. God is that Holy Mystery that bears the world up in its very existence. God exists as Being-in-Communion. There is no self-contained, divine individual residing in heaven far away from us. There is simply a dynamic movement of love that *is* God, in whom "we live and move and have our being" (Acts 17:28). This imaginative framework also has strong biblical roots. Saint Paul writes:

> *God's love has been poured into our hearts through the Holy Spirit that has been given to us. For while we were still weak, at the right time Christ died for the ungodly. Indeed, rarely will anyone die for a righteous person—though perhaps for a good person someone might actually dare to die. But God proves his love for us in that while we still were sinners Christ died for us (Romans 5:5-8).*

The Johannine literature also presents God not as an individual being to whose many attributes (for example, kindness, mercy, generosity) one can add "loving" but as Love Abiding.

> *Beloved, let us love one another,*
> *because love is of God; everyone who*
> *loves is begotten by God and knows*
> *God. Whoever is without love does not*
> *know God, for God is love....No one has*
> *ever seen God; [yet,] if we love one*
> *another, God remains in us, and his love*
> *is brought to perfection in us....God is*
> *love, and whoever remains in love re-*
> *mains in God and God in him....Those*
> *who say, "I love God," but hate their*
> *brothers or sisters, they are liars; for*
> *those who do not love a brother or sis-*
> *ter whom they have seen cannot love*
> *God whom they have not seen. The com-*
> *mandment we have from him is this:*
> *those who love God must love their*
> *brothers and sisters also. (1 John 4:7-*
> *8,12,16,20-21)*

What we have is a biblical tradition alive to the way in which love does not just describe an attribute of God but names the essential *way* in which God is God. This view of God as fundamentally relational and engaged in our world has been expressed in the insights of the many giants of our tradition. Saint Augustine captured something of it when he spoke of God as "closer to us than we are to ourselves." Saint Thomas Aquinas assumed this perspective in his presentation of creation, not as an event in the distant past but as an ongoing relation that describes how God even now stands as our Creator, sustaining all that is through participation in God's very being. Again, another diagram might be suggestive.

Saint Bonaventure captured this in his classic spiritual work, *The Soul's Journey into God,* a marvelous evocation of the way in which all of creation can be seen as a kind of sacrament. Julian of Norwich, a fourteenth-century anchorite (a spiritual person who lived alone in a hermitage attached to a church), affirmed it in her confident assertions that the doctrine of the Trinity was not an inscrutable cipher but rather an expression of God's pervasive presence and activity in the world. In her classic work, *Showings*, she has God speak: "See, I am God. See, I am in all things. See, I do all things. See, I never remove my hands from my works, nor ever shall without end."[3] And returning once again to Teilhard de Chardin, in that same text quoted earlier, he writes, "By virtue of the Creation and, still more, of the Incarnation, nothing here below is profane for those who know how to see."[4]

QUESTIONS FOR REFLECTION

Does your relationship with God lead you to confirm or reject this view of God as Divine Source and Superabundance of Love?

How does this view of God change the way you think about prayer?

Imago Dei:
We Are Made for Communion

This reflection on the doctrine of the Trinity leads us to another, closely related doctrinal commitment of the Church, namely that as humans we are made in the image and likeness of God. If God's very being is loving relationship, if God is Being-in-Communion, then it is also true that we image God insofar as we ourselves realize our truest identity as creatures made for communion.

Within each of us there is an inner restlessness, an insufficiency that impels us to engage our world, to forge meaningful relationships with others, to exercise our imaginations. The vitality of a human life can be measured by the intensity of one's desire. We know we are truly alive when we experience a drive for the more of life. I am not talking about false desire, the consumerist impulse, forged by modern marketing strategies. Here desire does not emerge from the spiritual wellspring within but is crassly manufactured and manipulated by companies eager to convince us that product X will finally satisfy that longing that they have planted within us. The expression of authentic human desire lies not in a desire for things. It is a much deeper impulse for human fulfillment.

Human desire is the source of our spiritual energy. It is what impels us to enter into relationship with others. We are driven into relationship by a deep sense that by connecting with another we might find wholeness. The Book of Genesis reminds us that we are created in the image and likeness of God. It is a way of saying that there is something vital within us that allows us to share or participate in God's life. When we are authentically human and give ourselves over to our deepest longing for communion, we are, at the same time, sharing in the life of God who is the Superabundant Source and Dynamism of Love itself. The difficulty is that for so long Christians have imagined that communion with God is a distinct spiritual quest that takes place alongside our other human commitments. Yet, as the account of the Trinity offered above suggests, we can distinguish but never separate the life of communion with God and the life of communion with one another.

This impulse for a life of communion exists in all of us. It flows from our being as persons. It is the fundamental motivation, for example, of the great humanists who claim nothing of belief in God but live selfless lives in service of their neighbor. To the extent that any human moves selflessly toward another, in vulnerability and trust, seeking the good of another, that person is realizing, however haltingly and imperfectly, a true vocation to a life of communion. When we humans surrender to this spiritual impulse for communion, we are, whether we know it or not, participating in the life of God who is Loving Communion. Let me offer a simple example.

A few days ago I came home from work and saw my wife Diana working on an art project with our six-year-old son, Brian. She was sitting at the table with him, the contents of our art box spread all over the table. They had planned on producing a poster of some sort, but Brian's own interests and enthusiasm were taking him in another direction—he wanted to make a model of an eagle with moving wings. Diana encouraged him to follow his creative impulses and helped him by procuring a paper-towel tube, some string, and various other supplies. She assisted him while always following his lead. Now, she had told me, just the night before, that she had a very ambitious list of errands that she needed to run the next day, but there she was, quietly setting aside her own anxieties about things to do in order to be present to Brian. It was an event of communion, communion with Brian to be sure, but as a genuine act of love it was, at the same time, communion with God who is the very source and dynamism of all love.

If we can affirm that all humans are invited by God to this life of communion, we Catholic Christians also believe that, as the living body of Christ, we are called as a Church to be a visible sacrament, a sign and instrument, of this communion. Vatican II put it quite clearly when it taught that "the Church, in Christ, is a sacrament—a sign and instrument, that is, of communion with God and of the unity of the entire human race" (*Lumen Gentium* # 1). The Church exists not for its own sake but to draw all of humankind into this twofold communion with God and with one another.

QUESTIONS FOR REFLECTION

Can you think of some instances in which you have entered into the life of communion with family members, friends, coworkers, or strangers?

Why do you think it is so difficult to identify God's presence in these moments?

Pastoral Ministry: Serving the Life of Communion

✠ ✠ ✠

L et me turn now to a new way of considering Christian ministry through understanding God as Loving Communion and through the belief that we are created in the image and likeness of God and as such are made for communion. Christian ministry is, in all of its many different manifestations, nothing more than service to the life of communion to which all are called.

The Minister As Mystagogue

With the integration of the catechumenate into the life and ministry of more and more Catholic parishes, many will already be familiar with the term *mystagogy*. In the catechumenate, mystagogy refers to the initiation of the neophytes, the newly baptized members of the community, into the mysteries of the faith. Yet we should not imagine that these mysteries of the faith are simply a collection of disparate truths to be learned and mastered. In reality, all the mysteries of the faith flow from our graced insight into God's offer of salvation, our belief in what God has done for us in Jesus of Nazareth by the power of the Holy Spirit.

There is, I believe, a mystagogical dimension to virtually any form of Christian ministry. It occurs whenever, through the sacraments, preaching, catechesis, or the basic ministry of personal presence to another, we invite others to encounter the Holy Mystery of God. Mystagogy also implies, however, that this triune God is to be encountered not in a separate, religious sphere of human existence maintained at a safe distance at the periphery of our daily concerns but rather at the very heart of human existence.

What I am suggesting here is that as Christian ministers we do not bring God to anyone. Any living, breathing, conscious human being has already had some experience of God, however veiled or confused it may have been. No human who has ever consciously walked this earth has been innocent of God's grace. All have been touched by grace even if we must accept the possibility that, in the deepest sanctuary of their hearts, it is possible to turn their backs on God. Our first task is not to bring God to a people radically unacquainted with the Holy Mystery but rather to help them discover the presence of God that has gone unnoted in their lives. For if the doctrine of the Trinity means anything, it means that long before we ever seek God, God has sought us, and long before we ever find God, God has already found us. When we minister to others, we must remember that God got to them before we did! Our task is both to draw from the riches of the Christian heritage to help name what people have, in some hidden and confused way, already experienced and also to allow the transformative power of the gospel to deepen people's experience of God. When we teach of both the reality of human sin and the reconciling love of God made manifest in Christ, these cannot be abstractions. They are terms, doctrines, concepts that will speak to people only to the extent that they name the gently wafting melodies and jolting dissonances already playing in their life stories.

Let me borrow an analogy that Father Michael Himes once used in a different context to explain how it is that sacraments cause grace. I am convinced that what he is saying of sacraments in fact names the mystagogical function of all explicit Christian ministry.

Imagine sitting in the waiting room of a dentist's office. You are paging through a dog-eared magazine with some recorded music playing in the background, though you are paying no attention to the music.

Indeed, were you to leave the waiting room and were someone to ask whether any music had been playing, you would reply with perfect candor, "No, I didn't hear anything." Shortly, another prospective patient enters, sits down near you, and after a moment inquires of you, "What is the name of that tune?" At that instant, for the first time, the music goes on *for you.*[5]

This is a basic responsibility of pastoral ministers, to call people's attention to the holy presence of God so often relegated to the background music of their lives. The poets seem to get this better than we theologians. Elizabeth Barrett Browning evokes the biblical story of Moses encountering God in the burning bush and being exhorted to remove his shoes before treading on holy ground. She writes in her narrative poem, "Aurora Leigh,"

Earth's crammed with heaven,
And every common bush afire with God;
But only he who sees, takes
    off his shoes—
The rest sit round it and pluck
    blackberries
And daub their natural faces unaware
More and more from the
    first similitude....
If a man could feel,
Not one day, in the artist's ecstasy,
But everyday, feast, fast, or
    working-day,
The spiritual significance burn through

The hieroglyphic of material shows,
Henceforward he would paint the globe
*   with wings,*
And reverence fish and fowl, the bull,
*   the tree,*
And even his very body as a man.[6]

This is the triune God, not a God standing on the periphery of our world but a God who shimmers in creation. And therein lies the problem. The common condition of humanity, call it original sin if you wish, is that we are all sitting around "plucking blackberries," unaware of the invitation to communion playing quietly in the background of our lives.

Let's flesh this out a bit. I have already suggested that at the heart of the doctrine of the Trinity is the simple yet profound biblical assertion, "God is love." Wherever there is authentic love, there is God. Yet there is more. We Christians believe that in Jesus of Nazareth's teaching and ministry, and in a special way in his suffering, death, and resurrection, God has revealed to us the distinctive shape, the characteristic pattern, rhythm, or even grammar, if you will, of the life of love. This too goes to the heart of Trinitarian doctrine—our conviction that in Jesus the triune being of God is revealed to us as perfect love. Consequently the ministry of mystagogy will involve helping those to whom we minister to name the moments in their lives in which they have entered into this rhythm of divine love. We must help them name the times in which, by dying to their own selfishness, egoism, and greed, and rising in simple yet courageous acts of love and care, they were in fact abiding in the love of God. Such graced moments might involve the primal care of a mother getting up with a child in the night or staying on the phone into the wee hours of the morning with a friend in difficulty, or a father changing his daughter's diaper, or an accountant going beyond the requirements of professional responsibility to take a personal concern in a client's hopes and fears. To believe that the Trinity reveals to us a God whose very being is characterized by loving communion means we must minister out of the conviction that in every event of human communion, in every authentic movement of love in which we postpone our preferences and desires as we attend to others, we share in the divine life of the triune God.

Thomas Merton once described a profound conversion he underwent in his sense of his monastic vocation. He was invited to broaden his idea of the monk as a separate, spiritual being and to embrace something quite different. Merton, one of America's most famous twentieth-century spiritual writers, recounted his dramatic conversion to Catholicism and eventual entry into a Trappist monastery in his classic work, *The Seven Storey Mountain.* In that work Merton viewed his spiritual pilgrimage as a pilgrimage away from the world into the special graced preserve of the monastery.

Yet later in his life he came to question this way of understanding his monastic vocation. He was in poor health and had to leave the monastery on occasion to go see a doctor in Louisville. During one of his trips to Louisville, he had a dramatic conversion experience on a street corner in downtown Louisville. There Merton gazed upon all of these strangers walking by and felt a mystical union with them. He realized that his view of the monk as a separate, spiritual person was not only an illusion but a dangerous illusion. He admitted that certainly there was something distinctive about being a monk, "for we belong to God. Yet so does everybody else belong to God. We just happen to be conscious of it, and to make a profession out of this consciousness." Later he would wonder at the miraculous dignity of the human person. "If only everybody could realize this! But it cannot be explained. There is no way of telling people that they are all walking around shining like the sun."[7] Merton has captured wonderfully the nature of mystagogy, the unique task of helping people discover that they are all "shining like the sun"!

Questions for Reflection

Do you think most of us really believe that we are all "shining like the sun"?

Are there aspects of our culture (for example, our reliance on technology or our tendency toward wasteful consumption) that make it harder for us to name the presence of God in the most ordinary aspects of our daily lives?

The Minister As Contemplative Witness to Life

There is a wonderful saying attributed to Saint Francis of Assisi, "Always preach the gospel—by words if necessary." Much of what we do as ministers flows out of who we are. This means that we must ourselves be living the life of communion. If we are to help others name the graced moments of communion in their lives, then we must ourselves be attentive to the experience of genuine communion in our own lives. This demands that the minister be something of a contemplative. This is a word that many of us associate more with saints or monks or some such thing. But I am using the word in a more basic sense. Mary, the mother of Jesus, was a contemplative. She pondered in her heart the wondrous things that happened to her. We must be contemplative in the same way. We must be quietly attentive to the movement of God's grace in our own lives, we must become ever more conscious of our own participation in the life of communion, if we are to help others in the movement toward communion.

But even more basically, if as ministers we are to give witness to the life of communion, we must also be healthy people. Saint Thomas Aquinas taught that "grace builds on nature." In other words, God's grace cooperates with and builds upon our basic human dispositions. We are better able to engage in Christian ministry if we are essentially healthy people. The problem is, how do we define *healthy*? We can speak, first, of the importance of a sense of self-esteem. It is impossible to minister effectively to others unless one operates out of a positive self-identity. This sense of self means that one is self-defined, not other-defined. Too many people minister out of a sense of what others expect of them rather than out of who they really are. Without being blind to human shortcomings, ministers must feel comfortable with who they are. They must have a healthy self-love and more importantly, a real sense of being loved unconditionally by God. They must be aware of their human failings without being overcome by them. They must be capable of meaningful, intimate human relationships. As Richard McBrien puts it,

Mentally unhealthy people almost inevitably project their own problems on to others. If a minister is pathologically guilt-ridden, that minister won't be satisfied until his or her pastoral "client" feels just as guilty about some form of human behavior as the minister feels.[8]

We must be particularly aware of the way ministry attracts codependents, those who need to be needed by others. Such people are seldom able to set limits in their ministry. They are often workaholics, prone to becoming enmeshed in ministerial relationships and prime candidates for burn-out. On the other hand, if we think of those people who have had the most profound effect on our lives, they are generally people who impress us not as perfect people but as healthy people who have a positive sense of their own self-worth and who help other people to feel better about themselves as well. These individuals are effective ministers not just because of their talents or their charisma but because people are drawn to their essential wholeness.

I recall my years as an undergraduate studying at the University of Texas. One great turning point in my spiritual journey was my encounter with a Catholic priest who was a campus minister. I was initially moved by my experience of him in formal ministry settings—by the manner of his prayerful presiding at the Eucharist, by his theological erudition in adult education programs, and by the passion of his preaching. Yet as I look back, I think he had far greater impact in less formal settings—informal conversation and storytelling in the Catholic student center lobby, playing racquetball. This priest's personal health and integration impressed me far more than his theological knowledge and erudition. So it often is in pastoral ministry. We minister as much by who we are as by what we do.

QUESTION FOR REFLECTION

We have spoken here about the importance of ministers being basically healthy people. How do you think psychological and emotional health relates to spiritual health?

The Minister As Prophet

As much as we believe that all humans, in the simple process of being human, encounter God in the daily run of events, we would have no need for Christian ministry if it were as simple as that. We are called, as creatures made in the image and likeness of God, to the life of communion. Yet we often reject this life of communion. We decide to remain in isolation, to make ourselves the ultimate reality, the center point of our universe. This is nothing less than the denial of our true humanity.

It has often been said that original sin is the one empirically verifiable doctrine in the Christian tradition! Because of its somewhat regrettable formulation in the writings of Saint Augustine, many contemporary Christians have been inclined to dismiss the doctrine of original sin. This is, I believe, a horrible mistake. For the doctrine of original sin names the indisputable experience of ourselves, when left to our own devices, as in some way estranged from the life of grace.

Returning to Father Himes's analogy, sometimes it is not just that we are ignoring the music but that we actively *choose* not to hear it by focusing too much on other things. It is often not enough to be *shown* God's grace, we must be transformed—we must be given eyes to see and ears to hear. Maybe Augustine—who described sinful humanity in terms of "disordered desire"— wasn't so far off the mark. He saw the fundamental human problem as one of desiring the wrong things for the wrong reasons. It wasn't that it was wrong to love the goods of creation (though he seemed to have had a bit of a blind spot where sexuality was concerned), it was our tendency to seek after the goods of creation as ends in themselves that could satisfy our spiritual cravings. I think of my own lust for techno-gadgets or my tendency to treat my wife as if she were brought into the world for the sole purpose of meeting my needs. I look at our whole ravenous consumer-culture that at every turn offers me some product to satisfy some manufactured need, and I wonder if Augustine wasn't on to something.

We do live in a world shot through with the presence of God, but we still need transformation, conversion if you will, that we might become more attentive, more conscious, and responsive to God's presence. The Bible refers to this conversion of heart and mind as *metanoia*. We cannot discover the God hidden in our daily lives until our desires are so reordered by God's grace that we truly want to, yearn to discover God. Robert Barron puts this situation well.

The proper starting point for any healthy Christian theological anthropology is a clear sense of the togetherness of original sin and likeness unto God, for without the first, metanoia is unnecessary, and without the second, it is impossible.[9]

The Christian minister must attend to the brokenness of our human condition, which we refer to as original sin. Because of our sinful human condition, we need conversion in order to see God. Consequently, Christian ministry makes use of the power of narrative (for example, gospel stories, stories of saints), religious art, ritual and symbol, and even Church doctrine to disrupt people's accustomed vision and invite them into new possibilities for seeing their lives and the world around them. We invite people into the distinctive Christian practices of our community—the liturgy, almsgiving, advocacy on behalf of basic human justice—because we believe that these elements in the great tradition help not just to illuminate the mystery of God already at work in people's lives but also to effect that transformation necessary for people to truly desire God's presence. This is why the mystagogical ministry invariably demands a prophetic dimension as well. As prophet the minister is called to speak out against anything that would stand in the way of the life of communion.

The Christian tradition has often conceived of sin as the transgression of law, be it Church law, natural law, or divine law. But there is another way of thinking about law. The early Christian community spoke of the account of God's work on their behalf in Jesus and the Spirit as the divine *oikonomia,* from whence we get our word *economy.* But the Greek word *oikonomia* is a composite of two other words, *oikos*, meaning *household,* and *nomos*, meaning *law* or *rule.* God's *oikonomia* or economy reveals to us how God would have God's household run. The *nomos* or law that is to be operative in God's household is the life of communion. This life is characterized by charity, justice, generosity, generativity, mutuality, inclusivity, and empowerment. From this perspective, sin names the intentional, culpable perversion or denial of this life of communion. It occurs whenever we treat others as objects, when we elevate ourselves as the ultimate reality. Sin happens when we act out of fear and demonize the stranger in our midst, whether that stranger be a person of another race, class, or sexual orientation. Sin names part of the woundedness of the human condition. Moreover, these obstacles to communion often are systemic or institutional in character. That is, there are clearly institutional structures that perpetuate injustice, that deprive people of their fundamental human rights and their dignity as children of God. The minister as prophet must be willing to speak out against these injustices.

This human woundedness is not limited to the moral sphere of life. We are wounded by much more than sin, and these wounds, like sin, can also inhibit our capacity to live in communion with God and neighbor. We can learn much from the social and behavioral sciences on this score. Sociology helps us appreciate the significance of the social structures in which we are formed and nurtured, structures like the family and educational institutions. The impact of single-parent households, gangs, teenage pregnancy, drug abuse, and bad schools on a person's capacity for healthy human relationships has been well documented. Psychology complements sociology by mapping out the wounds that mark the human psyche in its fragile journey toward psychological maturation. The recent sociopsychological developments in systems theory and our understanding of addictive processes suggest that substance abuse and codependency can manifest behaviors that are life denying. Cultural anthropology highlights the important role that ethnic and cultural structures and value systems play in shaping our relationships with others. Moreover, what makes the human experience of our brokenness so complex is that so often both sinful and non-moral factors (for example, in addiction) are inextricably interwoven. When an alcoholic husband beats his wife, how do we separate the moral from the non-moral factors?

Because of the brokenness of human existence, the Christian minister must combine mystagogy with prophecy. For though it is important to help people name the events of graced communion in their lives, it is also vital that we be able to recognize and name the human experiences of brokenness, sinful and non-sinful, that damage or impede our capacity for communion. This prophetic ministry has its foundations in the Old Testament, for example, Amos's denunciation of the callous disregard of the wealthy for the poor. Jesus also exercised this kind of prophetic ministry. He knew well the multitude of ways in which the capacity for human communion could be squelched and even extinguished by poverty, ostracism, and the life of privilege and power. Jesus was fearless in his condemnation of every worldly power that quenched the human spirit. We must follow him in fulfilling this necessary prophetic function.

QUESTION FOR REFLECTION

Do you think our feel-good society makes it harder for people to exercise a prophetic ministry?

The Minister As a Compassionate and Healing Presence

There is a special need for us to understand ministry as service to the life of communion when we minister to those who suffer. For suffering, in its most acute form, is an assault on the very possibility of a person's being able to experience communion. Wendy Farley speaks of the experience of what she calls "radical suffering."

Radical suffering is present when the negativity of a situation is experienced as an assault on one's personhood as such....This assault reduces the capacity of the sufferer to exercise freedom, to feel affection, to hope, to love God....In radical suffering the soul itself has been so crippled that it can no longer deny evil. The destruction of the human being is so complete that even the shred of dignity that might demand vindication is extinguished.[10]

People who are broken down by suffering often speak of being overwhelmed by a sense of powerlessness, helplessness, or meaninglessness. They have lost their capacity for authentically loving and caring relationships, not because of sin but because of the searing effects of pain and suffering. The difficulties they face have been transformed from everyday problems into genuine crises. Problems at times are little more than a nuisance, at other times they can be quite imposing, but they do have recognizable solutions. Crises are something altogether different. When a person is in a crisis, as in times of great suffering and tragedy, what is needed is not a solution but a *presence*. Scott Gustafson writes:

> *A crisis challenges the very resources that are normally used to solve problems. Quite often a divorce or the death of a spouse is a crisis because the person who is absent was a means of resolving difficult problems like raising children or maintaining financial or even emotional stability. In other*

words, a divorce or death is a crisis because that which is normally used to solve a problem is undermined.[11]

This may be the most fundamental insight of pastoral ministry. Too often those of us in pastoral ministry come to our ministry precisely because we are problem solvers. We have been affirmed as fixers or peacemakers in our own families. We eagerly brandish our problem-solving skills in our ministries. Earlier we discussed the importance of a minister's fundamental healthiness. Yet here it is vital that ministers be aware of their own woundedness as well. Having accepted the reality of suffering and loneliness in their own lives, the very woundedness of ministers can become a strength. These wounds can become a font for Christian ministry, a place where we turn inward to fuel our compassion and solidarity with the physically, emotionally, and psychologically broken in our world. This has been one of the central insights of Twelve Step programs and their use of mentors. The mentor helps the addict, not from a position of moral superiority, but precisely as another pilgrim on the way to wholeness. As Henri Nouwen reminded us, out of a humble recognition of personal brokenness the minister may become a "wounded healer."[12]

What makes understanding ministry to the suffering so difficult is the fact that those who suffer frequently come to us seeking answers. People want to find meaning in their suffering. They want to believe that there is some purpose to it, something that can satisfactorily explain why it has been visited upon them. Yet, as Christian ministers we often cannot answer the why of suffering, as much as we may want to. While those who suffer often profess to want a reason for their suffering, what they *need* may be something quite different. What those who suffer may need, whether they are aware of it or not, is not so much a solution but a community that will assist them in negotiating the burdens of their pain. If much of the destructive power of suffering is derived from its meaninglessness, then what is needed is a minister who can assure the sufferer of the meaningfulness, not of the experience of suffering itself, but of our lives in general. People must be able to tell the story of their suffering in the presence of a minister who can tell the story of God's compassionate presence in the person of Jesus.

This ministry of compassionate presence is itself a kind of healing ministry. Our understanding of the minister as a healer takes its inspiration from the ministry of Jesus. His ministry brought freedom from the power of those forces that could distort the human movement toward another in the life of communion. Too often our view of the healing ministry of Jesus has focused on the miraculous. But perhaps the greatest healing that Jesus offered came not from the regeneration of withered limbs or blind eyes but from Jesus' offer of unconditional acceptance extended toward each person he met. Jesus' relationships were characterized by a probing, perceptive attentiveness to the other. How much healing transpired in Jesus' offer of friendship to Mary and Martha, second-class citizens by virtue of their gender? Was there a healing that transformed illiterate laborers into fearless witnesses to the

Christian faith? If we are to believe the gospels, Jesus wrought healing as much by his personal presence to others, a presence that was attentive, affirming, and empowering, as by dramatic, miraculous deeds. The pastoral minister today must share in Jesus' work to bring wholeness and reconciliation, never forgetting that the most powerful vehicle for personal healing is that of a compassionate presence and attentiveness to others.

QUESTION FOR REFLECTION

Why do you think it is so hard for many of us to resist the temptation to fix people's problems?

The Minister As a Person of Hope

At some point or other, every person who does ministry comes to question the effectiveness of their work. They find themselves preoccupied with the difficulty in assessing the fruits of their labor. What is lacking, all too often, is an appreciation of what we might call the eschatological character of the life of communion. What this means is that the fullness of the life of communion will only be ours in the *eschaton*, in the consummation of history when God's *shalom* shall reign, when "they shall beat their swords into plowshares" (Isaiah 2:4) and when the lion lies down with the lamb. (See Isaiah 11:6.) Until that time, it will be our lot to travel through history as pilgrims, spinning tales of blessing and loss, and blessing *in* loss. In this world, on this journey, the fullness of that communion for which we were made will always elude us. Within human history our ministry can only reap partial victories and a multitude of apparent failures. Our survival as ministers depends on our possession of genuine Christian hope grounded in prayer and nurtured in Christian community. Ministry must always resist the allure of the numbers game, the accounts of souls won for Christ.

The need for hope in Christian ministry is poignantly displayed in Jon Hassler's novel, *North of Hope.* The novel is about a middle-aged priest struggling to rediscover his priestly vocation. He suffers from what he calls a "spiritual leak." He is assigned to a mission on a Native American reservation in Minnesota and arrives, spiritually dying, only to find a dying remnant of a community. He soon realizes that he was assigned there, not to minister to a community but to preside over the quiet death of a small mission that had outlived its usefulness.

At the same time, he discovers that the reservation's resident doctor is married to the woman with whom the priest had been in love some twenty years earlier, before he entered the seminary. She is living a life of despair in a destructive marriage. For her the reservation and all that it represents exists "north of hope." The turning point comes when an old family friend comes to the priest for confession and admits that she had, with the purest of intentions, misled him when she told him years before that his mother's dying wish was that he become a priest. In point of fact, it had only been her wish that he would *want to* become a priest. Upon hearing her confession, he is surprised to discover that this revelation does not devastate him, as it might have earlier. He realizes that he has come to terms with who he is and what he can do. He rediscovers his ministry in the healing power of his simple presence before others. In the end he recognizes that there is no place north of hope, for "hope goes wherever you want it to."[13] This hope is possible only by accepting one's modest place in God's providential plan.

Like Hassler's priest, as persons of hope, ministers can only avoid burn-out to the extent that they remain rooted in the rightness of the particular place in which they find themselves. This requires a confidence in the mystery of God's plan and a humility about the ways in which we contribute to that plan. When ministers possess Christian hope, they are able to minister out of a fundamental confidence that humankind's future and the future of God will someday be one.

QUESTIONS FOR REFLECTION

Have you ever experienced pressure to produce numbers or offer tangible demonstrations that your ministry has been a success?

How do you sustain hope in your ministry?

Conclusion

✠ ✠ ✠

The great Jesuit theologian Karl Rahner once made the provocative claim that "The Christian of the future will be a mystic or he or she will not be a Christian at all."[14] By "mystic's" he did not mean those who had extraordinary ecstatic visions or some such thing but Christian's who had cultivated a sense of God in their daily lives. I have tried to suggest in this presentation that the doctrine of the Trinity teaches us, if nothing else, that our God is no distant, unrelated being who must be called into our world, as it were. Our God is the Superabundant Source and Dynamism of Love and, as such, is the very ground and atmosphere of our very being. This God is Being-in-Communion, and our task, as creatures made in the divine image, is to cultivate the life of communion with God and one another as the very fulfillment of our human destiny. As pastoral ministers, we must be mystagogues and prophets, contemplatives and agents of divine compassion, persons of hope and above all servants to the life of communion for which all are called by God. We are ministers who are invited to lead people through the riches of our tradition to a discovery of this God, to walk with them on the path of spiritual transformation in which, through participation in a community of faith, they might become mystics familiar with the "genuine experience of God emerging from the heart of existence."

ENDNOTES

1. Congregation for the Clergy, *General Directory for Catechesis* (Washington, D.C.: USCC, 1997), 95 (#100).
2. Teilhard de Chardin, *The Divine Milieu* (New York: Harper & Row, 1969), 65-66.
3. As quoted in Elizabeth Dreyer, *Manifestations of Grace* (Wilmington: Glazier, 1990), 109.
4. Teilhard de Chardin, *The Divine Milieu,* 66.
5. Michael Himes, "Making Priesthood Possible: Who Does What and Why?" in *Priesthood in the Modern World: A Reader,* ed. Karen Sue Smith (Franklin, Wis.: Sheed & Ward, 1999), 41.
6. Elizabeth Barrett Browning, "Aurora Leigh," *Mrs. Browning's Complete Poetical Works* (Cambridge Edition, Boston and New York: Houghton, Mifflin and Co., 1900), Book VII, lines 821-26 and 857-64.
7. Thomas Merton, *Conjectures of a Guilty Bystander* (Garden City: Doubleday, 1966), 156-57.
8. Richard McBrien, *Ministry* (San Francisco: Harper & Row, 1987), 55.
9. Robert Barron, *And Now I See: A Theology of Transformation* (New York: Crossroad, 1998), 22.
10. Wendy Farley, *Tragic Vision and Divine Compassion: A Contemporary Theodicy* (Louisville: Westminster John Knox Press, 1990), 53-55.
11. Scott Gustafson, "From Theodicy to Discipleship," *Scottish Journal of Theology* 45 (1992), 219.
12. Henri J.M. Nouwen, *The Wounded Healer* (Garden City: Image Books, 1972).
13. Jon Hassler, *North of Hope* (New York: Ballantine, 1990), 498.
14. Karl Rahner, "The Spirituality of the Church of the Future," *Theological Investigations,* vol. 20 (New York: Crossroad, 1981), 149.